Andrew Young speaks at a press conference at the United Nations.

ANDREW YOUNG
Freedom Fighter

By Naurice Roberts

 CHILDRENS PRESS, CHICAGO

Picture Acknowledgments

UPI: United Press International—cover, 2, 6, 8, 10, 13
(2 photos), 15 (2 photos), 16, 17, 18 (2 photos), 20, 21, 22,
23, 25, 26, 27, 28 (2 photos), 30, 31

Office of the Mayor, Atlanta, Georgia—Cover

Library of Congress Cataloging in Publication Data

Roberts, Naurice.
    Andrew Young, freedom fighter.

    (Easy-to-read biographies)
    Summary: A brief biography of the clergyman, civil rights worker, legislator,
first black United States Ambassador to the United Nations, and current Mayor
of Atlanta.
    1. Young, Andrew, 1932-   —Juvenile literature. 2. Legislators — United
States — Biography — Juvenile literature. 3. Ambassadors — United States —
Biography — Juvenile literature. 4. United States. Congresses. House —
Biography — Juvenile literature. 5. United Church of Christ — United States —
Clergy — Biography — Juvenile literature. [1. Young, Andrew, 1932-
2. Statesmen. 3. Afro-Americans — Biography] I. Title. II. Series.
E840.8.Y64R62 1983   973.92'092'4 [B] [92] 83-7633
ISBN 0-516-03450-2

    3   4   5   6   7   8   9   10   R   92   91   90   89   88   87   86   85

ANDREW YOUNG
Freedom Fighter

Beneath a portrait of her husband, Coretta Scott King, the widow of
Dr. Martin Luther King, Jr., (far left) joins hands with Vice-President Walter
Mondale, U.S. Ambassador to the United Nations Andrew Young, and the
Reverend Mr. Martin Luther King, Sr. to sing "We Shall Overcome."

WE SHALL OVERCOME, WE SHALL
    OVERCOME,
WE SHALL OVERCOME, SOMEDAY.
OH, DEEP IN MY HEART, I DO BELIEVE,
WE SHALL OVERCOME, SOMEDAY.

The words are from the popular
song of the Civil Rights Movement
in the 1960s. This was a time in
our country's history when black
people marched for equal rights
and opportunities.

Many people helped make the
song popular. Andrew Young was
one of them.

Andrew "Andy" Young, Jr., was
born March 12, 1932, in New
Orleans, Louisiana, the older of two
sons of Andrew Young, Sr., and
Daisy Fuller Young.

A sharecropper home reflects the poverty found in many farming communities in the Deep South.

The kids in the neighborhood called him "the rich kid" because Andy came from a well-to-do family. His father was a dentist and his mother was a schoolteacher.

It didn't matter that his neighbors were white and poor. Andy and his brother, Walter, played games with the children on Cleveland Street where they lived.

Black and white children didn't play together that much in the segregated South. They also went to separate schools. They sat in separate places in movies and restaurants. Andy and his brother didn't like this. Segregation meant they couldn't do all the things their playmates did.

But Andy and Walter did many things their poor neighbors didn't do. Their parents took them to places like New York City. There they went to nonsegregated restaurants, parks, movies, and other places. They did all the things they couldn't do in the segregated South.

Andy was small. Because of his size, he never made any sports team in high school. Once his father was worried that Andy couldn't take care of himself. He hired a boxer to teach Andy to fight.

But Andrew decided there was another way to settle a disagreement. Talk it out instead of fighting! He believed what his father had always told him, "Don't get mad, get smart!"

Dr. and Mrs. Young also taught Andy and Walter never to hate or dislike anyone because of his or her skin color. The Young family was very religious.

Andy was always curious. He wanted to know about everything.

He was a great reader. If he wasn't reading, he could be found swimming.

Dr. Young was concerned about his son's future. He wanted Andy to be a doctor or a dentist. But Andy didn't know what he wanted to become.

In 1947, he graduated from Gilbert Academy, a private high school in New Orleans, at the age of fifteen. He wanted to go away to college, but his parents thought he was too young. So, for a year he went to Dillard University, a black school near his home. In 1949, Andy transferred to Howard University, another black school, in Washington, D.C.

At Howard, Andy was still younger and smaller than his classmates. In his senior year, he made the track and swimming teams. But he still hadn't made up his mind about a career.

In 1951, when he was nineteen, Andy graduated with a bachelor of science degree. While his classmates were preparing for marriage, graduate school, or jobs, Andy returned home to an uncertain future in New Orleans.

On the way home from school, Andy talked to a young man who was on his way to Africa to be a missionary. He was very impressed.

That summer Andy volunteered to work for six months with the United Christian Youth Movement.

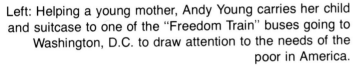

Above: Dr. Martin Luther King walks a group of school children to their newly integrated school. Andy Young is at the left.

Left: Helping a young mother, Andy Young carries her child and suitcase to one of the "Freedom Train" buses going to Washington, D.C. to draw attention to the needs of the poor in America.

He didn't know it then, but this was the beginning of his lifework.

Andy loved working with teens of all races. He knew it was important for people to help each other. He thought it was the best job anyone could do in life. By the time he had completed his volunteer assignment in Connecticut, he had made an important decision. Andrew Young decided to be a minister.

He enrolled at Hartford Theological Seminary, a school for ministers in Connecticut. There he learned about the world's great religious leaders. He especially liked Mohandas Gandhi, the famous religious leader of India, who led his people in their struggle for independence from Great Britain. This was the first time Andy Young learned of nonviolence. No fighting back. The student minister liked this way of thinking.

Each summer, the students went to different cities throughout the country to preach and work. In 1952, Andy began working in rural Marion, Alabama. The people liked him. So did Jean Childs, a student studying education at Manchester

Left: Pope John Paul II met with Andrew Young when he was U.S. ambassador to the United Nations. Right: Andrew and Jean Childs Young

College in Indiana. Andy liked her, too. They had a lot in common. Their goals in life were the same. Jean was also a religious person and wanted to help people.

The next year, the young minister went to Europe to help refugees. Although far away, he hadn't forgotten the pretty lady he had met in Marion, Alabama. Soon, Jean Childs became Mrs. Andrew Young.

15

As a Congregationalist minister, Ambassador Andrew Young officiated at the marriage of tennis champion Arthur Ashe to Jeanne Marie Moutsussamy.

In February, 1955, Andrew Young received a bachelor of divinity degree and was ordained a minister. Now he had a real plan in life.

Young and his wife worked in poor rural communities in Georgia. The area needed a strong minister. There was much to do.

A group of black teachers attempting to register
to vote were stopped by local police officers.

After a while, Andy decided to
talk about more than religion. He
talked about voting. Blacks didn't
vote in the South. It was just too
dangerous. But Andy was not
afraid to face danger. Andy
encouraged his people to vote.

The Youngs thought about their
work and the new child they had to
protect. They strongly believed
their faith would protect them. So
their civil rights work continued.

By now Andrew Young had
heard about the Montgomery bus

Dr. Martin Luther King (left) led the bus boycott. When protesters (above) sat in seats marked for whites only, they were arrested.

boycott in Alabama. Blacks decided not to ride the bus until they could sit anywhere they liked. A young minister, Dr. Martin Luther King, Jr., organized the boycott. This was the beginning of the Civil Rights Movement. Dr. King and Andrew Young would soon work together.

Although things were happening in the South, the rural communities where Andy worked were slow to act. He became disappointed and decided to leave. He accepted a job in New York with the National Council of Churches. The work

18

with young people was enjoyable and challenging. But the challenge was not as great as working in the Civil Rights Movement. Andy and Jean knew the job would be dangerous, but they returned to the South.

Settling in Atlanta, Georgia, with Jean and their three daughters — Andrea, Lisa, and Paula — Andrew Young directed a voter registration project. He worked with Dr. King and the Southern Christian Leadership Conference (SCLC) and the Congress on Racial Equality. Dr. Martin Luther King also lived in Atlanta. So did Andy's brother, Walter, who was now a dentist. Soon Andy Young joined Dr. King and SCLC.

Dr. Martin Luther King, Jr., Ralph Abernathy (center), and Andrew Young organized and led civil rights demonstrations and marches.

Andy Young became one of the strong leaders of the organization and a close friend of Dr. King. He had an important job. He worked behind the scenes, usually organizing marches and planning demonstrations. Even though many civil rights workers were jailed and beaten, they believed in Dr. King's philosophy of nonviolence. Andy believed it, too. No fighting back!

Protesters march down Constitution Avenue in Washington, D.C.

In August, 1963, over 200,000
people went to Washington, D.C.,
for a great march on Washington.
Dr. Martin Luther King, Jr., gave
his famous "I Have A Dream"
speech on the steps of the Lincoln
Memorial. It was a peaceful
demonstration. Andrew Young was
glad to be part of this exciting
event.

Andy Young and
Ralph Abernathy
speak to the press
the day after Dr. Martin
Luther King, Jr.
was killed.

Although the struggle for civil rights was important, another conflict was stirring. Now attention was shifting to the war in Vietnam. Like Dr. King and many civil rights leaders, Andy Young believed the war was wrong.

Now the antiwar and civil rights people demonstrated together. The marches continued. On April 4, 1968, the marches suddenly stopped. Dr. Martin Luther King, Jr., who was in Memphis,

Tennessee, to lead a demonstration,
was shot and killed. Andrew Young
was with him. Like millions of
Americans, he cried.

Andy Young began thinking
about the future and how he could
help make changes for black people.
The answer was politics. He talked
with other leaders and decided to
run for Congress in 1970. There
had been no black congressman from
the South since after the Civil War.

Although Andy Young was popular, many were afraid of his opinions. He lost the election. At the same time he became friends with Georgia's governor Jimmy Carter and his family.

Believing strongly that he could win, the civil rights leader decided to run again in 1972. Andy Young of Georgia and Barbara Jordan of Texas, became the first two black congressional representatives from the Deep South since the 1880s.

A freshman congressman has a lot of work to do. Andy Young learned quickly. He had a new job and a new addition to his family — Andrew Jackson Young III. The baby boy was nicknamed "Bo."

Congressman Andrew Young with his wife Jean and son Andrew III.

Congressman Young did a good job. He was reelected in 1974. He was also well liked by his colleagues. If there was a serious problem or argument, Andy Young was called. He knew how to solve problems and make things right for both sides. Andrew Young was also a member of the Congressional Black Caucus. This was a group of black legislators.

President Jimmy Carter met with UN Ambassador Andrew Young to discuss African affairs.

During this time, he became very interested in African affairs. The congressman visited Africa several times. In 1976 he was elected to his third term. At the same time, another Georgian, Jimmy Carter, was elected president of the United States.

President Jimmy Carter asked his good friend and supporter Andrew Young to be United States ambassador to the United Nations.

Andrew Young addresses a UN Security Council meeting.

If he accepted the post, Andrew Young would become the highest black official in the country. He would be the first black to hold this position. Many of Andy's friends didn't want him to leave Congress. They didn't think the UN position was important.

After much thought and prayer, Congressman Young accepted the job. He seriously wanted to get involved in international affairs

Ambassador Andrew Young was very interested in African affairs. He did everything he could to promote peace while fighting for the political freedom of the African people.

and help foreign countries better understand the United States. He thought being an ambassador was a good opportunity to do this.

Ambassador Young made friends for the United States all over the world, especially in Africa. He often spoke out on different issues and problems. Sometimes his statements caused disagreement and arguments. A few government officials thought he should resign. But President Carter always supported his friend.

One day, the ambassador said something in public that was considered embarrassing to the United States. After much confusion, Andrew Young resigned in September, 1979.

The former ambassador and civil rights leader started an organization called Young Ideas. This group did not make money, but helped groups and organizations work on public issues in the United States and other countries. He also wrote a newspaper column for two years.

Then Andrew Young decided to
run for public office again. He ran
for mayor of Atlanta, Georgia, and
won. Andrew Young took office on
January 4, 1982.

Andrew Young has been a
freedom fighter all his life, as
clergyman, youth worker, civil
rights leader, congressman,
ambassador, and now as mayor.
He's received a number of awards
and honors for his work, including
the Presidential Medal of Freedom,
which is our nation's highest

Mayor Andrew Young addressed the U.S. House of Representatives in 1982.

civilian award. Mayor Young continues working and struggling for equal rights and opportunities for all people.

Many things have changed since he began his work. He realizes there is much to do. Andrew Young remembers the civil rights movement and the popular song he sang. He still sings that song and honestly believes in the words that one day "WE SHALL OVERCOME!"

ANDREW YOUNG

1932	Born March 12, New Orleans, Louisiana
1947	Graduated from Gilbert Academy at age fifteen
1951	Graduated from Howard University in Washington, D.C.
1952	Began working as student minister in Marion, Alabama
1954	Married Jean Childs, June 7
1955	Graduated from Hartford Theological Seminary (became ordained minister)
1961	Joined Dr. Martin Luther King, Jr., and the Southern Christian Leadership Conference
1963	Helped organize march on Washington
1964	Worked on passage of Civil Rights Act
1965	Worked on Voting Rights Act
1968	Helped organize Poor People's Campaign
1972	Elected to U. S. House of Representatives, first black congressman from Georgia in 101 years
1974	Reelected to Congress for second term
1976	Reelected to Congress for third term, appointed United States ambassador to the United Nations by President Jimmy Carter
1979	Resigned as U. S. ambassador on September 23
1980-81	President of Young Ideas; columnist for the *Los Angeles Times*
1981	Elected mayor of Atlanta, Georgia

ABOUT THE AUTHOR

NAURICE ROBERTS has written numerous stories and poems for children. Her background includes work as a copywriter, television personality, commercial announcer, college instructor, communications consultant, and human resources trainer. She received a B.A. in Broadcast Communications from Columbia College in Chicago where she presently resides. Her hobbies include working with young people, lecturing, and jogging. *Andrew Young* is her first book published by Childrens Press.